The Question & Answer Book

DISCOVERING FOSSILS

DISCOVERING FOSSILS

By Wendy Rydell
Illustrated by Ray Burns

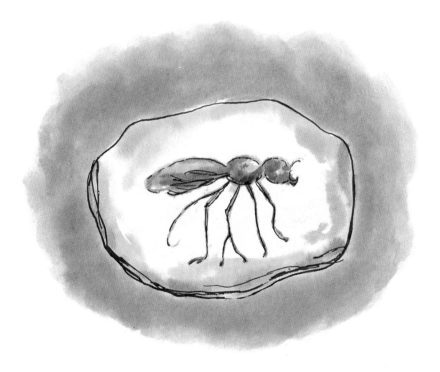

Troll Associates

Library of Congress Cataloging in Publication Data

Rydell, Wendy.
    Discovering fossils.

    (Question and answer book)
    Summary: Answers questions about the frozen, petrified,
molded, imprinted, or otherwise preserved remains of
prehistoric life forms which guide scientists in their
study of early plants and animals.
    1. Paleontology—Juvenile literature. [1. Paleontology.
2. Fossils. 3. Prehistoric animals. 4. Questions and
answers] I. Burns, Raymond, 1924- ill. II. Title.
III. Series.
QE714.5.R93 1984   560   83-4832
ISBN 0-89375-973-2
ISBN 0-89375-974-0 (pbk.)

Printed in the United States of America
10   9   8   7   6   5   4   3   2   1

How old is the earth?

Our earth is billions of years old.
Scientists believe it was formed about
four and a half billion years ago.
People have lived on the earth for
only a small bit of that time—
perhaps two and a half million years.
Yet we know that long before us,
there were other forms of life.

What forms of life lived long ago?

There were tiny, one-celled plants and towering, tree-like ferns. There were microscopic animals and gigantic dinosaurs. We know about these ancient plants and animals even though they died out long before the earliest people lived. We know about them because they left records— strange, exciting records, buried deep within the earth. These records are called *fossils*.

What is a fossil?

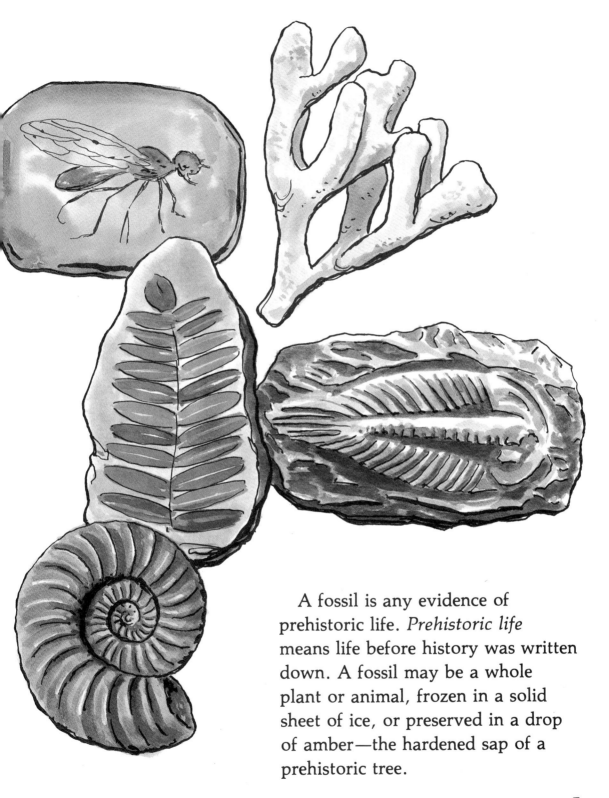

A fossil is any evidence of prehistoric life. *Prehistoric life* means life before history was written down. A fossil may be a whole plant or animal, frozen in a solid sheet of ice, or preserved in a drop of amber—the hardened sap of a prehistoric tree.

Or a fossil may be the petrified remains of an ancient plant or animal. *Petrified* means turned to stone. This happens when buried remains are slowly dissolved, or washed away, and replaced by minerals.

A fossil may be a *mold* or *cast*. This happens when the buried remains of a plant or animal are dissolved, but *not* replaced by stone-hard minerals. Nothing is left but a hollow outline in the surrounding rock.

A fossil may be nothing more than
a *print* that is made in solid rock that
was formed from prehistoric mud.
The print could be the footprint of an
extinct animal or the burrowing trail
of a prehistoric worm. It could be the
imprint of a delicate, 300-million-
year-old leaf.

What must happen before a fossil can be identified?

First, a fossil must be preserved, so it is not eaten, decayed, or destroyed. It must be protected for a long, long time. Then it must be unearthed and discovered. Finally, it must be recognized as a fossil and properly identified.

What do fossils tell us?

It seems amazing that any fossils are ever discovered and identified. But they are—in enough numbers and kinds for modern fossil hunters to solve many of the mysteries about life in the past.

Unfortunately, it took a great many years before people realized that there even *was* a mystery, and that fossils could help to solve it. Early people believed that life on earth—and even the earth itself—had been the same since the beginning of time. So when early people accidentally stumbled across fossils, they did not know what to think. Countless fossils were ignored, reburied, or even destroyed.

Who first discovered the importance of fossils?

About 2,500 years ago, a few Greek thinkers suggested that these strange objects might actually be the remains of creatures that had lived on earth a long, long time ago. But everyone laughed at such an idea.

Almost 2,000 years later, in Italy, workers were digging a canal far from the sea. They uncovered all sorts of strange, stone-hard shells. Leonardo da Vinci—the great artist and inventor—quickly grasped the importance of these unusual shells. He correctly thought that they were the remains of ancient forms of sea life. Then he reasoned that if sea creatures once lived there, an ancient sea must have once covered what was now land. But what had happened to the sea? Why had it disappeared?

It was not until more than 300 years had passed that da Vinci's questions were answered. In 1795, a surveyor named William Smith had just begun to lay out a path for a new canal in England. He discovered something very strange. As he dug deep into the earth, he noticed that the rocks formed layers—or *strata*—one on top of the other, something like the layers of a cake.

He noticed that in some places, the strata were flat and even. In others, they curved up sharply, as if some powerful force had pushed them up.

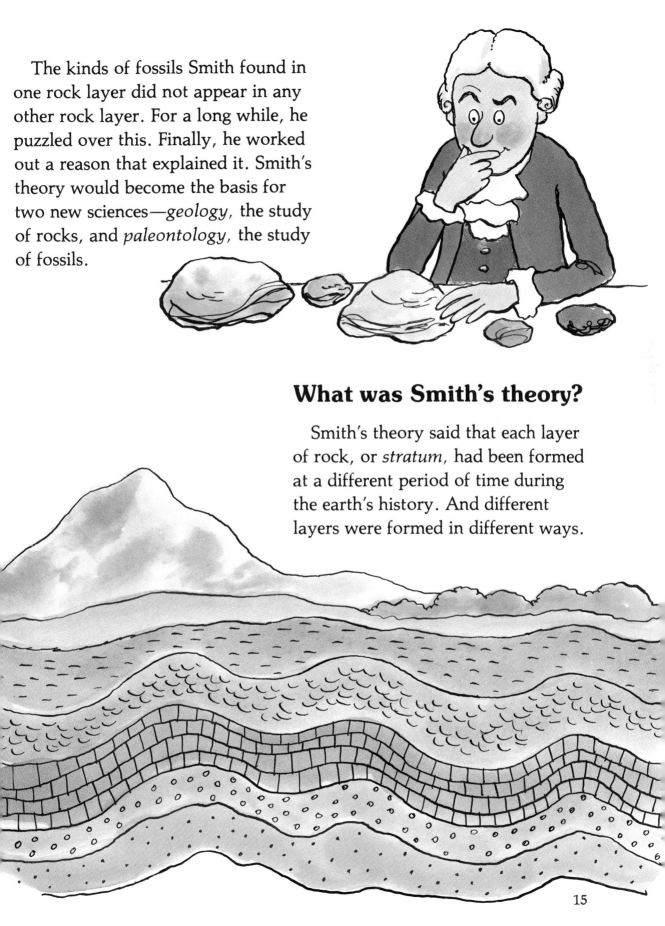

The kinds of fossils Smith found in one rock layer did not appear in any other rock layer. For a long while, he puzzled over this. Finally, he worked out a reason that explained it. Smith's theory would become the basis for two new sciences—*geology*, the study of rocks, and *paleontology*, the study of fossils.

What was Smith's theory?

Smith's theory said that each layer of rock, or *stratum*, had been formed at a different period of time during the earth's history. And different layers were formed in different ways.

15

One of the layers was made of a kind of rock called limestone. Limestone is made of a mineral that is found in sea water. Smith correctly guessed that the layer of limestone had been formed at a time when a sea covered that part of England. A great force from deep inside the earth must have raised the ocean floor and caused the sea to drain away.

When the sea disappeared, sand must have covered the land, because the layer above the limestone was made of sandstone. Later, plants must have appeared in great numbers, because the next layer was made of coal. Coal is formed from the remains of ancient plants.

How did Smith "date" the fossils in each layer of rock?

Smith's theory also said that the fossils in each layer were the remains of plants and animals that were alive when the layer was forming. So any fossils found in the sandstone layer must be the same age as the sandstone. And any fossils found in the limestone layer must be the same age as the limestone.

Thanks to William Smith, fossil hunters could now date their "finds," if they knew the age of the rock in which the fossils were buried. And geologists could now identify matching rock layers even when these layers appeared in widely scattered parts of the world.

What are the "four great eras"?

After Smith's discovery, scientists began charting the way the earth had changed in prehistoric times. To make their task easier, they divided prehistoric time into four great periods of time called *eras*. These eras were named: beginning life, primitive life, middle life, and recent life. Each era was based on the kinds of fossil life that were uncovered. And with each new fossil discovery, scientists were able to solve a bit more of the ancient mystery of what kinds of life had once existed on the earth.

What can a single fossil tell us?

Today's fossil experts can often "read" a fossil as easily as most people read their newspapers. A single, fossilized leg bone can tell a great deal about the kind of creature that once stood on it. A tiny fossilized shell can give a clear picture of the creature that once lived inside it. It may even give a clue about how and why that creature died.

What are some famous fossil finds?

Most fossil finds are nothing more than fragments—single pieces of skeletons or broken imprints on shattered bits of rock. Like detectives, *paleontologists*, scientists who study fossils, must put these pieces back together again. Often, they must reconstruct missing parts, based on what they think a prehistoric creature looked like.

But every now and then, an amazing fossil find is made—a complete, fossilized creature is discovered—and our knowledge of prehistoric life takes a giant leap forward. One such discovery was made in the early 1900s, in northern Siberia.

A hunter and his dogs were walking along the *tundra*, the deeply frozen ground of Siberia. Suddenly, part of a hill ripped away in a noisy landslide. Sniffing and barking, the dogs ran to the part of the hill that was still standing. They began to tear away at something inside it.

When the hunter reached the hill, he could not believe his eyes. There stood a huge woolly mammoth—an elephant-like beast at least 25,000 years old! Somehow, the entire mammoth—flesh and all—had been frozen inside the tundra. Released by the landslide, the giant beast looked just as it did on the day it died.

20

What sort of story can fossils tell us?

Paleontologists in California once unearthed a large
number of fossil bones from the La Brea tar pits.
When they sorted out the bones, they discovered that
they belonged to four different prehistoric animals—
a mammoth, a huge saber-toothed tiger, a large vulture,
and a giant wolf.

From the position of the bones, the scientists put together a story that may tell what happened there thousands of years ago.

The scientists reasoned that the mammoth probably became trapped in the sticky tar pit. As it struggled to get free, it was seen by the saber-toothed tiger. The ferocious cat pounced on what must have looked like an easy meal. But the mammoth lashed out with its powerful trunk, and the tiger fell backward into the tar.

Soon the vulture swooped down on the two dying animals. But the tiger, struggling and clawing the air, pulled the bird down. Finally, a hungry wolf tried to make a meal of the dead creatures. And it, too, slipped into the sticky deathtrap.

Slowly, all four animals sank deep into the tar. Only their fossilized bones were left to tell the tale of how they had lived and died.

Have the bones of previously unknown creatures been discovered?

Yes, sometimes fossils of previously unknown creatures are discovered by fossil hunters. Just such a discovery was made in 1922.

It was then that paleontologists discovered a kind of dinosaur graveyard in the side of a sandstone cliff. Among the fossils they collected were at least seventy-five skulls and several complete skeletons of an unknown kind of horned dinosaur. This strange creature was later named *protoceratops.*

The fossilized bones were from
dinosaurs of all ages—from very
young to very old. And something
else was there, too—a nest of
fossilized protoceratops eggs with
baby dinosaurs still inside them!

This marvelous discovery allowed scientists to trace the entire life span of the protoceratops, from birth to death, in perfect detail. But even without such a complete discovery, paleontologists have been able to trace the evolution of many other prehistoric creatures. *Evolution* is the growth, change, and development of various kinds of animals.

What more do we still need to know?

The fascinating mystery of prehistoric life is not yet completely solved. Many more fossil discoveries, especially of the earth's earliest life, still need to be made. And some very important ones might well be made by amateur fossil hunters—like you— out for a day of fossil collecting.

What does it take to be a part-time fossil hunter?

It takes some knowledge of sedimentary rocks. These are the kinds of rocks in which fossils are most often found. It takes some planning to locate a good fossil-hunting spot. It also takes a bit of adventurous spirit and a lot of luck.

27

To be an amateur fossil hunter, you need little more than a hammer, a chisel, and a knife. The hammer is used for chipping hard rocks. The chisel is for prying out and splitting softer rocks. The knife is for carefully loosening the soil around each fossil.

These tools and any fossils that you find can be carried in a small canvas bag. But protect every fossil you discover by wrapping tissue paper or cotton around it before you carry it away.

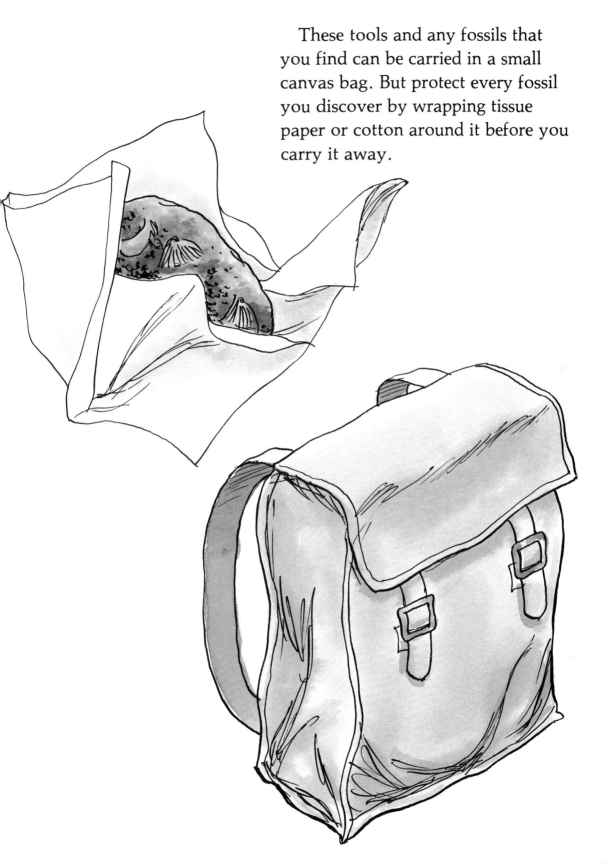

It is always a good idea to carefully note the exact location of each fossil find. Then, after the fossil treasure is placed in a tray or box, you can begin the exciting job of identifying it. This might be done by comparing it to illustrations of fossils in encyclopedias and other reference books.

What kinds of fossils will you find?

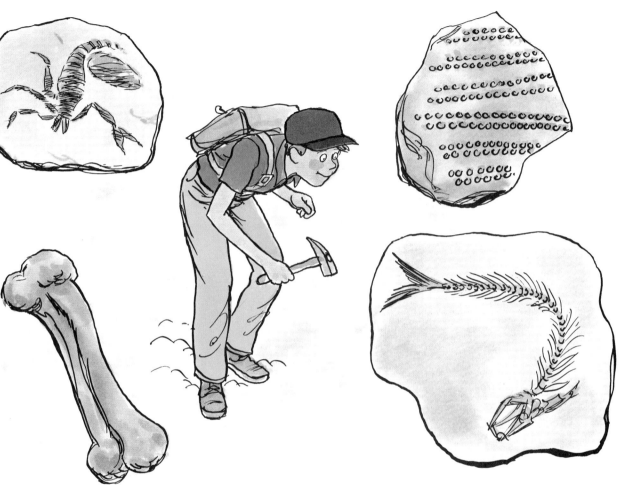

No one can say for sure. You might search and search, yet find nothing at all.

But you might find a bit of prehistoric bone or the print of an ancient plant. You might come across a fossilized shell of some extinct sea creature or a petrified piece of a prehistoric tree. You might even find a gigantic tooth or a tiny insect in a drop of amber.

Who knows?

No one can say exactly when or where the next great fossil find will be made. It might be right in your own neighborhood. And no one can name the fossil hunter who will make the next important discovery. Who knows...it might even be you!